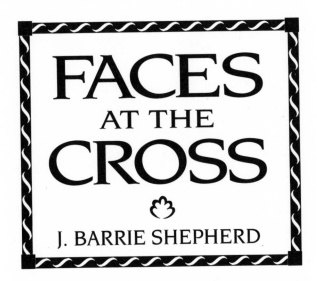

FACES
AT THE
CROSS

J. BARRIE SHEPHERD

FACES

AT THE

CROSS

A Lent and Easter
Collection of
Poetry and Prose

J. BARRIE SHEPHERD

UPPER
ROOM BOOKS
NASHVILLE

FACES AT THE CROSS

Cover Design: Susan Scruggs
Interior Design: Jim Bateman
First Printing: January 1995 (5)
Library of Congress Catalog Number: 94-61266
ISBN: 0-8358-0715-0

Printed in the United States of America

I dedicate this book

to the people of my present parish,

The First Presbyterian Church

in

The City of New York;

to the community we serve

in Greenwich Village;

and to the city

to which we have ministered

since 1716.

Also by J. Barrie Shepherd

Seeing with the Soul
  Daily Meditations on the Parables of Jesus in Luke

The Moveable Feast
  Selected Poems for the Christian Year and Beyond

A Pilgrim's Way
  Meditations for Lent and Easter

A Child Is Born
  Meditations for Advent and Christmas

Praying the Psalms
  Daily Meditations on Cherished Psalms

Prayers from the Mount
  Daily Meditations on the Sermon on the Mount

Encounters
  Poetic Meditations on the Old Testament

A Diary of Prayer
  Daily Meditations on the Parables of Jesus

Diary of Daily Prayer

Faces at the Manger
  An Advent-Christmas Sampler of Poems,
  Prayers, and Meditations

A Way for the Pilgrim: A Book of Meditations

CONTENTS

PART TWO

PREFACE

Each year as I make my way through Holy Week, I find myself wondering about the people involved in those terrible-wonderful days in old Jerusalem. From the maids in Caiaphas's courtyard to that high priest's servant whose ear was off and on again, it seems, before he had time to miss it; from the widow with her two mites to the owner of that donkey Jesus borrowed for his entry to the city; these days are filled with incidents in which ordinary people encountered Jesus, for better and for worse.

What were those people thinking of, worrying about, hoping for, fearful of, as events drew toward their climax? How could they explain to themselves, justify, or make sense out of the words they spoke, the actions they had a part in? What did they make of the One who gave himself into their hands and never seemed to give up loving them, no matter what they did? "Part One" of this book uses the poetic imagination to explore what might have been the emotions, confusions, rationalizations, and insights of those who stood among that crowd on the hill called Golgotha. Some of these people, as well as many of those whose names and roles are far more widely known today than they ever were two thousand years ago, shape the content in this section.

"Part Two" presents a selection of verse for Lent and Easter. Many of these poems have appeared over the past twenty years in *The Christian Century* and other publications. I have arranged these poems in the form of a pilgrimage, tracing the Lenten journey from Ash

Wednesday, through the weeks of discipline and preparation, to the intensity of Holy Week, to the church's holiest and most joy-filled day of days.

Like my earlier book, *Faces at the Manger*, this work combines something of the flavor of an anthology with that of an original work. It is my hope and prayer that this book will prove to be a companion on the Lenten way. It should be used, not as a substitute, but as a catalyst for the reader's personal devotion. It has to be undergirded with persistent and perceptive searching of the scriptures. Used in this way it may, by grace, lead the reader to find and claim a place on Calvary, to recognize his or her own face among these *Faces at the Cross*.

WERE YOU THERE?

It was an evening of glorious music.
Even the stars in the velvet vault above
seemed to grow more radiant
as the night unfolded its treasures.
The audience,
spread across the lawns of the great city park,
sank deeper into the enchanted web
being woven by the great orchestra and soloist.
All too soon it was time
for the final encore of the evening.
The diva returned to center stage.
The orchestra rested their instruments.
And the silence yielded to one solitary voice
breathing the soul of her people and her faith:
>   Were you there when they crucified my Lord?
>   Were you there when they crucified my Lord?
>   Oh! sometimes it causes me to tremble . . .
>   tremble . . . tremble.
>   Were you there when they crucified my Lord?

There are few pieces of music, if any,
with more power to capture, to enthrall,
to move a group of human beings
than that simple, passionate
and profound cry from the heart.
Some of its secret resides,
to be sure, in the music;
few melodies have the ability
to pierce the soul as this one does.
Much of the power of this song
comes from its history in the life

and suffering of the African American people.
But what sets this song apart, even from all
those other moving and evocative spirituals
of the African American heritage,
is the question that it asks,
that searching, searching question:
> Were you there
> when they crucified my Lord?
> Were you there?

Who *was* there?
So many of the familiar "Sunday School picture scenes"
> from the Gospels—
Jesus teaching by the seashore,
blessing the children, healing the sick,
feeding hungry multitudes,
teaching his chosen disciples—
can leave us wishing we had been there,
dreaming of some kind of time machine
in which to be transported back
for a brief visit to the shores
and hillsides of Galilee.
As an avid summer fisherman
in the waters off the coast of Maine,
I, for one, would love to have had a hand
in that miraculous draft of fishes.
But Golgotha—
place of the skull—
that other hillside,
just outside the city walls,
where three great criss-crossed stakes,
all smeared and streaked with blood and gore,
stand stuck into the earth and braced and wedged
to hold their dreadful burdens up to God
or to whoever now can bear to see
those gray, contorted faces;
who wants to make that trip,

who wants to stand amid that gloating,
guilty, grieving crowd?
Were you there?

The scriptures have an answer for us,
they tell us who was there
in some of the most dramatic,
descriptive writing
in all of literature.
No detail seems to be spared;
four hundred and seventy verses
it takes the four Gospel writers
to cover the narrative of that fearful night and day—
        Last Supper, Gethsemane, capture and trials,
        scourging, crucifixion, and death.
The scriptures tell us who was there.

The disciples were there.
Although when needed most,
when called upon to be what he had taught them,
trained them to be, they all disappeared.
"The Jews" were there.
Although, despite some of the writing
and much of later history,
they can hardly, as a race,
be shouldered with the blame for this.
Jesus and his followers
were all Jews too, after all!
The religious leaders were there.
Ready to preserve at any and all costs
their institutions and traditions,
their hard-won establishment,
from the disturbing threat of new ideas,
fresh understandings, radical proposals.
The Romans were there.
Pilate, their pliable Governor,
and the ever-dependable legionaries,

ready to do whatever dirty work
was passed down the chain of command.
The people were there.
Swiftly transformed
from a cheering throng hailing their Messiah
to an ugly mob bellowing for his death.
The women were there.
Powerless to do anything
beyond witnessing from afar
and then doing their best to clean up the mess
when it seemed all was over and done with.
The victims were there.
Innocent and guilty, the penitent one,
the defiant one—all three
victims of the failure of a system,
of our race, to learn to live in peace,
with truth and justice.

Yes, the scriptures tell us who was there.
Yet beneath the written testament,
reading between the lines, we can perceive,
if we are open, a far wider audience,
a much more all-encompassing throng
that stood about that cross on Calvary.
We see the officialdom of every age:
those bureaucrats who simply do their job
but in so doing consign the weak
and the unfortunate to death;
leaders ready to commit judicial murder
rather than risk their own position
of authority and power.
We see those ever-practical souls
who would invoke the theology of expediency,
claiming God's endorsement
for their cunning plots and schemes.
We see those who,
in the name of peace and quiet,

set aside the high demands of morality and law.
We see bigots there and butchers, brutes,
those who find a twisted satisfaction
in the witnessing of human suffering and pain;
we see cowards there and crooks and,
if we will look with fully opened eyes,
we see ourselves,
knowing this is wrong,
is evil, is perverse,
wanting to cry out,
to intervene,
to bring proceedings to a halt,
and yet afraid,
because we also know that if we do,
if we utter one brief murmur of mild protest,
we risk joining him up there,
we risk "taking up the cross to follow him."
And what would that gain, after all,
just another senseless death?
So we keep quiet,
while we hate ourselves for doing so.

Were you there?
Were you there when they crucified my Lord?
I was there. You were there.
We were there.
Faces at the cross.

Part 1

THE FACE OF SIMON OF CYRENE

How I got involved in this
I'll never know.
I was on my way into the city,
trying to finish up my business there
and get on the way back home before the Sabbath,
when I heard a commotion in the streets.
Next thing I knew I was in the middle of a mob
leading, dragging three poor souls out of the city
to their deaths by crucifixion.

Just as I was trying to work my way
toward the edges of the crowd,
a rough hand grasped me by the shoulder,
span me around, and I saw I was in the hold
of one of the Roman legionaries from the fort.
He led me to the officer in charge, saying:

> Here's a fine strong fellow, from the country
> by the look of him. Maybe he's from Galilee
> and a follower of the Jew-King here. He'll do
> to carry the cross.

And, before I could protest,
they had shoved me under an enormous wooden cross
that had been lying in the road and prodded me
into lifting it, bearing it down the street.

Well, it doesn't do
to argue too much with these Romsan soldiers.
For one thing, they don't speak our language,
most of them, and for another,

they are apt to turn on you
and fling you in their cells to cool off overnight.
Besides, if they really thought I was a follower
of one of these unfortunates,
then who's to say where I might end up
if I'm not careful?

I couldn't help noticing, however,
even staggering as I was under that cruel load,
that the one whose cross I bore
was quite different from the other two.
They looked like typical malefactors,
no-goods, with ragged garments,
shaggy hair and beards
and a wild and cunning look
about their faces.
The third one—my one—
seemed a gentler soul.
He clearly had been more severely beaten,
yet I never heard one word of complaint or self-pity.
The other two were making their share of noise,
and more, proclaiming their innocence,
screaming to the crowd to save them
from these foreign troops, and then to God
to deliver them in their innocence.
He had a kind of dignity about him,
for all his ragged garb,
his bruised and blood-streaked body
made me wonder what his crime had been;
he didn't strike me as a criminal.
Then I saw the placard they were carrying along
to nail up on his cross.

King of the Jews

it said, in all three languages,
so I guess he must have committed some kind
of political, or maybe even church-related crime.

As we walked,
or rather stumbled, through the streets,
he met my eye, from time to time,
and I felt drawn to him.
He was obviously sorry I had to bear his burden,
but more than that, it seemed as if
he had some kind of secret word, or gift,
to share with me, something he wanted to say.

It was then I noticed
he was mouthing something,
trying to get words across to me above the din
echoing back and forth along those narrow city ways.

God loves you.

Finally I figured it out.
Was he simply saying thank you
for the help I had been compelled to give?
Was he, in his most unblessed state,
trying to pronounce some kind of blessing on me?
Or was he telling me some news?
That was the way he seemed to be regarding it,
as if it were the latest,
the hottest piece of news that ever was.

You know something,
as he said it, with those deep eyes of his,
as he looked across at me, crook-kneed beneath my load,
and, failing though he was, bellowed these words
over the clamor of the street:

God loves you.

Some kind of blessing did descend.
I felt suddenly sure of who I was and what I was doing.
I felt that, of all the places in the world,

there was no place I would rather be
than here, compelled to bear this awful weight.
I felt as if my life, maybe, had moved
across all of its years toward
this moment and these eyes,
toward these words that simply said:

> God loves you.

So I'm standing here,
all thought of business long forgot,
waiting for another glimpse of those eyes,
another moving of those lips,
another chance to hear that news
that shook me to the core,
still shakes me now as I recall it,
and heals me deep in places
where I never dreamt I needed to be healed.

What will I tell my wife when I go home?
How can I explain what happened to me
to the boys, Alexander and Rufus?
Can I find a way to share with them
the news he passed along to me today?
Can I find a way to shape my days
around that simple message he is dying
to make live in me just now?

> God loves me.
> God loves you.

That's the word.

THE FACE OF NICODEMUS

What if he sees me?
Will he realize why I am here?
Will that uncanny gift of his
to peer inside my head,
read the conflicts there—
all the competing hope and fear
he showed me on that night when
I stole out to meet him, asked him
about this second birth he speaks of—
will that gift enable him to understand
that I stand here among my lofty colleagues
from the Sanhedrin, not to scoff or to condemn,
not to gloat with them about the bitter ending
we have put to all his gentle words of peace,
but to share, to join my prayers with those
who seek to ease somehow the awful burden
that he bears for us, for everyone,
up there on that grim tree?

I'm still not sure what light it was
that drew me to him under cover of the night,
those many moons ago now.
Might it have been the free and soaring spirit
that he spoke of, blowing where it wills,
that blew me, flustered and confused,
but eager somehow, thirsting, starving,
famished for a word of life,
blew me clear into his searching presence,
into the presence of a mystery,
a mystery shot through, like rippling silk,
shot with the living color of the truth?

This second womb he spoke of,
a womb which, like the womb of night,
can hide all that disfigures and distorts,
but more, can wipe all that away forever
and leave one fresh and clean as a cord-cut babe
with its whole life before it,
this other birth has laid its hold
upon my days since then so that,
waking or sleeping, my hands reach out
to grasp what he held up before my disbelieving,
doubting, fearing eyes.

I had so much to lose, you see.
A position on the court of the Sanhedrin,
the long tradition of my family and lineage,
too much esteem and influence to set aside,
forsake in order to follow in the steps
of a young country preacher, whose words,
for all that they intrigued me,
were troubling to my associates in authority.
At least, that was my decision.

So now I have to stand here,
pretend that I belong among these mockers
and these fools, these life-long scholars of salvation
who cannot see the irony of their own cry:
         He saved others,
         now he cannot save himself.
I have to stand here praying that the blood
and sweat across his brow will blind him to my presence,
praying too that my companions will not sense
my deep discomfort, even real agony
over all that takes place here before us.

There's old Joseph over there,
Joseph from Arimathea.
I always wondered where he stood,

thought I glimpsed him once or twice
on the edges of the crowds surrounding Jesus.
He too looks not a bit triumphant,
cast down, rather, by this ghastly scene.
Could I risk a word or two with him about Jesus?
Might the two of us prevail, use our joint influence
to have this thing cut short,
the unnecessary suffering brought to a halt
and a decent burial arranged for?
I know I've got some spices,
myrrh and aloes, set aside.
If nothing else, they could be used
to sweeten his last resting place.
Yes, I'll take it up with Joseph
the moment I can catch his attention
without making it all seem too obvious.

Funny, we spoke so much about birth,
he and I, that time we met,
and now I stand witnessing his death.
Funny, that as I caught Joseph's eye just now
that self-same feeling stirred inside me
as if a flame had touched,
a wind had gusted,
a child had kicked its way
toward its bursting from the womb.
Womb, tomb, our first and last extremities.
How could they ever meet?

Here comes Joseph now,
picking his way toward me
with a strange, determined,
even defiant look about his eyes.
Well, we shall see.

THE FACE OF A BYSTANDER

The things these Romans do to people!

Only this morning I set out,
a joyful psalm light on my lips,
making the last stage of my *Aliyah*,
my annual "going up" on holy pilgrimage
to the great temple of King Solomon.

Then, just before the city gate
I ran headlong into an enormous throng,
shoving me aside, then off the highway,
shouting, jostling, jeering, even tossing rocks,
as three convicted criminals were led out
to be nailed up on Golgotha.
The Roman soldiers round them
paid no attention to the crowd;
they marched as if in stiff disdain,
arrogant eyes fixed straight ahead,
avoiding all unnecessary contact
with our alien and, to them, fanatic race,
pausing only to prod the stumbling victims,
staggering under the weight of heavy crosses,
trying to move them faster up the road
toward their place of final torment.
        Let's get this over with
was what their gestures said in silent eloquence.

The folk were packed so tight,
the way so narrow that I had no other choice
but to be swept along and swallowed up
into that surging mob.

At one point I found myself
quite close to the three malefactors
and able, whether I really wanted to or not,
to give them a look over.

By this time,
what with the flogging by the Palace guard,
the crushing weight of the crosses,
and their continual falling down,
they were a sorry sight,
all bruises, sweat, and mud,
with blood already flowing free
and a gaze of wordless horror
fixed across their haggard faces.
Although one of them, the one
that ended up there in the middle,
seemed more concerned about the crowd
than fearful for himself.
He wore a mocking crown of cruel thorns
that had been driven low across his brow
so that the blood ran down his cheeks
and through his beard.

Just before the crowd engulfed
and swallowed me again
I caught a glimpse,
behind the matted hair,
of gentle, deep-set eyes,
eyes that seemed to pick me out and hold me,
understand that I was there unwillingly,
through no decision of my own,
that I was anything but a full participant
in this scene of dreadful butchery.
Then he was lost to me and yet,
when an avenue of escape opened up
a moment later, I did not take it,
could not leave that face,

those eyes alone,
without one sympathetic gaze,
without someone to respond to him
from among this callous mob.

And here I've been all day
waiting to catch his eye from time to time,
hoping, yes believing somehow that my being here
has made a difference, however slight,
has eased, at least, the awful loneliness
of hanging between earth and heaven,
waiting for the final gift of friendly death.

And so my pilgrimage
will have to wait another day
for its completion.
Strange how a day can end up so very different
from the way that it began,
the way that it was planned to be.
All the same, despite the horror of this scene,
despite this desperate place,
these coarse and brutal people all about,
I know a sense of holiness as I look upon his face.
I feel as if I stood already far within the temple,
yes, even in the holiest of holies.
I sense an odd conviction that the *Aliyah*,
that my "going up," is now completed
and my pilgrimage is done.

The things these Romans do to people!

THE FACE OF MAGDALEN

So did we love him wrongly, after all?
Could this grim horror have been prevented?
Might it have never had to happen,
if we, if I, had only figured out the right way
to respond to all the love we found,
and felt and feasted on in him?

His love was unconditional,
always there for me,
even when he might have been provoked,
annoyed, or disappointed
in something I had said or done,
an attitude to others.
Our love—
mine I *do* know about, for sure—
our love was always eager to possess.
We loved him, those of us who got close enough,
just as one might love a thing of beauty,
cherishing its grace and loveliness,
needing to reach out and grasp it,
have it be at our disposal,
ready to be enjoyed at any moment.

He said his love, God's love,
was just like that,
was always there for us,
shining on us like the sun,
and would never let us down.
We didn't have to make it ours,
lock it up and throw away the key,

couldn't do that anyway,
because God's love can not be held,
can only be received and passed along.

And right then,
when we were with him,
when he was telling us all this,
we could believe it, at least I could.
Trouble was,
he wasn't always there
and then the doubts began again.

You see, love is such a basic thing,
being loved is so important that,
if you can't be certain sure God loves you
then you just have to love yourself.
You have to watch out all the time
to make sure you don't get hurt.
You have to realize,
accept the fact that everybody else
is busy loving their own selves.
So you can never fully trust them
because finally, when a life is on the line,
they will want it to be yours,
rather than theirs.

See what happened to him.
See where his God-love got him in the end.
Do you suppose he still believes in it up there?
Do you think, with all the hurt and hate
he's seen these past few hours,
he still hangs on to what he taught,
and walked and worked at with us
all those weeks and months
that seemed to be leading toward forever
till they ended with a crash?

Now even the two thieves
are cursing at him in their desperation.
Why must they pick on him?
Don't they know?
His suffering's as bad as theirs,
and he's done nothing to deserve it.
Just listen to them argue,
even up there when all is lost
they can't agree on anything it seems.

What's that?
One of them is defending Jesus,
asking him to bless him in his death?
And Jesus is assuring him of paradise,
blessing the legionaries too
as they gamble for his seamless robe.

What love is this?
What wondrous love is this?
Of all the miracles
I've witnessed these past months,
the miracle he brought about in my own life,
this is the richest, truest of them all.
Even death, this cruel, bloody death,
cannot quench the flow of God's love in this man,
this man I love, and learn to trust in God by.

His body weakens fast now.
It's getting harder and harder for him to breathe.
And yet the love, God's love in him,
goes on, and on, and on.
It's almost as if that love can never die;
almost as if, beyond the grave,
God's love in him will still go on,
will still be with me giving strength
to live the way he did,

even to die the way he dies.
God grant it may be so.

One thing I know,
whether we loved him wrong or not,
he loved us right.

THE FACE OF BARABBAS

What am I doing here
when I could be down at Jonas's tavern
celebrating with the rest
this freedom I had never thought to see again?
Should have been me up there, you know,
me wriggling against the brutal wood and nails,
me gasping out however many minutes of agony are left
before the lungs collapse, the heart gives out,
or the Romans finish me off.

That ambush, over a week ago—
surely someone tipped them off—
when we swooped down on the baggage train
and were swooped down on from behind
by a troop of Pilate's cavalry,
from that moment on I knew
that this was it for me,
that my long string of crafty moves
and lucky breaks had finally come full circle
and reached its bitter end.

The jailers
were so certain I was done for
that they eased off,
softened up on me these last few days,
even gave me food fit to be eaten,
clean water to drink and wash in.
Didn't sleep much though,
having pretty much given up hope myself,
being convinced this dawn would be the last one
I would see this side of kingdom come.

Then, right at the darkest hour,
when the chills come on you,
and then the sweats,
all that commotion and din in the court,
priests and soldiers screaming for silence,
and Pilate's shrill voice, high above the rest.

Whom do you wish that I release to you?

And the mob,
yelling my name again and again;
although how they even knew that I exist,
let alone my name—Barabbas—
is more than I have been able to figure out.

The iron door flung wide,
the chains removed—none too smoothly, by the way—
and a Roman legion boot square in my back
as they pitched me out onto the street.
I lay there several minutes,
too dazed to understand what had happened,
then it was up and onto my wobbling feet
and shambling through the alleys like a madman,
desperate for distance,
just in case they changed their minds.

After I slowed down for breath
I heard the yelling of the crowd again,
moving this time, or so it seemed,
tracking the same way I was headed,
toward the city gates,
hooting and jeering, laughing and cursing,
but there was wailing mixed in too,
and the solid tramp of marching feet.

Before I knew it they were all about,
cramming up the street from wall to wall

and leaving no escape.
I felt trapped, shut in all over again.
And then I saw him,
the one they've crucified instead of me.

He could scarcely walk,
let alone carry that huge cross.
The whips had sliced his ribs and back
and thorns had ripped his head
so that he looked more like raw meat
than a human soul.
But his face was still amazingly unmarked.
And then I saw his eyes.
They looked at me and wouldn't stop
but pierced inside, saw clear down to the core.
He knew me, knew who I was,
I'm sure of that, lay money on it.
Yet there was no anger there,
those eyes were terrible
not with rage, or even anguish,
but with compassion and great tenderness.

I couldn't leave.
Walked among that mob
as if I were enthralled, under some spell.
Absolutely had to see this thing through to the end.
He prayed for them, actually prayed for the soldiers
as they pinned him to the wood,
wouldn't take the numbing wine, "death's ease,"
they offered to him on the sponge,
and even spoke kind words of comfort to Demas,
my old comrade, who was right up there beside him.

"King of the Jews" they're calling him,
or so it reads above his head.
Well at least he purchased freedom,
removed the Roman captor's yoke

from the shoulders of one Jew today.
Strange this new freedom doesn't feel so free.
Some new and irresistible compulsion,
stronger than chains or iron bars,
will not let me quit this gruesome place
until he finds his own release,
until I know the reason for his death,
the meaning of that look he gave me,
the secret of the quiet, gentle power
in those words he spoke to Demas.

The soldiers have his robe,
they are dicing for his garments.
Perhaps, while they are arguing,
I can steal a word with those women over there
who appear to have been his followers.
Perhaps one of them can tell me,
can help me understand,
why he died and why I live,
what I must do to find,
at last, my freedom.

THE FACE OF JUDAS

Things got out of hand,
I mean, completely out of hand.
Ever since that day at Caesarea Philippi
when that idiot, Peter, said Jesus was the Christ
and then he started all that talk
about having to be killed,
and taking up the cross,
and us following in his steps;
ever since it began to dawn on me
that his plan was not to be a victor,
but a victim, not to win in this world,
but in some other I have never understood;
ever since they started coming to me secretly
with all their plots and schemes
either to remove the taint of treason
from his preaching,
or to ease him to the wings,
take over leadership,
and then,
move against the heathen Romans;
ever since all that
I have dreaded it would ultimately come to this.

Why couldn't he listen,
when I tried to reason with him
on the road and at the supper table?
Why couldn't he see the grim realities
that stared him in the face?
The temple crowd will never sit by passively
while he endangers the convenient arrangements

they have made with Mother Rome.
The insurrectionists could not abide
his otherworldly kingdom talk,
his lack of direct and decisive action.
And the people wanted to be led.
One way or the other,
what they asked of him was action,
not advice, programs or promises,
and certainly not the preaching of God's grace
and gentleness of soul.

Maybe if I forced his hand . . .
That's what they whispered to me,
maybe if I found a way to trap him,
put him in a spot where he had no other option
except to act,
strike out in self-defense, if nothing else,
then this whole enterprise,
this daring revolution we have worked on
for almost three long years,
could be finally brought to a head,
a climax, and concluded with a victory.
And they persuaded me.

So now I lurk here in the shadows,
to watch my friend, my leader, teacher,
dreamer of my brightest dreams,
perish in disgrace and bitter agony.
Somehow it all got turned upside down,
almost as if he knew my plans,
accepted them, up to a point,
but used them to fulfill
his own ideas of destiny,
not mine.

So that now,
as I stand here,

witnessing his cruel death,
I can see, again, what I had lost,
the one I loved and chose to follow
back among the hills and valleys of our Galilee.
I see clearly, but too late,
what has been veiled from me these shadowed weeks,
the clarity of love and lasting truth
that clings to everything he does
and says and is.

Pray God he doesn't see me,
that I'm far enough away
not to be recognized by those wounded eyes
that used to shine with love for me
and hope.
Pray God that Peter and the rest,
Mary too,
especially Mary,
do not pass this way
and recognize, accuse, condemn,
treat me as the outcast I must be to them,
and to myself,
from this day forward.

What is this pouch of silver that I clutch?
What is this life that I must linger in
knowing what has been sold and bought,
betrayed by me this day?
This fate is more than I,
than anyone can bear.
I must be rid of it.

THE FACE OF JOHN

He was giving us to each other.
That's what it was all about.
At first I thought he was delirious,
driven out of his mind by pain,
but now I see, I finally understand.
That's what he meant to say
with those odd words to Mary, his mother,
and to me:
   Behold your son . . .
   Behold your mother.

Who would have thought he could say anything at all.
So weak and torn and desolate he looks,
half-dead before they even got him here,
with all that whipping and tormenting,
stumbling along these streets,
the very same ones he rode through
in his triumph just five days ago.

I couldn't bear to watch them hammer in the nails.
So I took Mary and the women out of sight
to spare them at least
that particularly painful anguish.
Those hands that were so supple,
so skillful, strong to craft things in the shop,
so gentle to bring healing, food and comfort,
so eloquent in gesture and debate,
now hanging limp and useless,
pinned to the very wood he used to work with,
incapable of movement.

And yet he spoke to us just minutes ago.
Looked full at Mary,
with an amazing tenderness,
and moving his poor wounded head
toward where I was standing next to her,
he told her she should take me for her son.

Then it was my turn,
all said so patiently and slow,
pronounced as if he was revealing
his own last will and testament.
Come to think of it,
perhaps he was.

It strikes me now that,
in that act,
in giving us to each other,
Jesus has been disposing of the only,
and also the most important possessions
that are left to him.
His garments have been stripped away
and bartered for.
There is nothing else
he ever cared to call his own.
What Jesus cares about is people,
those close to him,
those who know need and pain,
even those who crucify him now
as he prays God's forgiveness for them.

So that, in giving us to one another,
he was simply taking care of those he loves,
entrusting us into each other's keeping,
and bidding us,
in his inimitable way,
to take care of each other
until his return.

I suppose that could be true for all of us,
I mean, for James, John, and Andrew,
Peter and the rest, wherever they are,
Jesus' last gift to us is one another,
the love and trust of this community we share
and have become together over the months and miles
since first he called us by the lakeside.

Some of his gift will not be easy to accept.
There are those of us, I'm sure, who
will not be eager to have any part of it—
what about Judas, for example,
where does he fit in,
or does he?
Jesus was always giving surprising gifts.
Maybe this last will be the most surprising yet,
most challenging too.

I wonder how much longer.
They say sometimes they hang up there for days,
but this being Passover, and tomorrow the Sabbath,
I believe they'll want to get it over with
and the bodies away before sundown.
Pray God they let us have his body;
it will mean so much to Mary, Magdalen too.
They may well find some consolation
in preparing him for burial.

I must speak to one of the soldiers.
Their centurion looks a sympathetic sort—
for a Roman officer anyway.
Pity the man who has to do what he does.
Pity the man who has to obey orders
such as his have been today.
Maybe he'll understand.

THE FACE OF CAIAPHAS

Sabbath is drawing closer.
Why can't they finish them off now,
get the corpses down before the feast begins?
Why prolong the suffering of these wretches?
Why permit their presence to pollute our Passover?
I must send someone to Pilate
to make sure he understands the laws,
surrounding this our holiest of Feast Days,
appreciates the sacrosanct traditions
that must be observed.

On the whole, though,
Pilate acted rather well
throughout this sad affair.
Once we made clear the crucial point
that this fool had called himself a king,
there was little else he could do,
no alternative really but to have him put to death.
If the word had traveled back to Rome,
(and we would have made certain that it did)
that Pilate had ignored
such a threat to Rome's imperium,
he could have found himself condemned,
instead of this ignorant peasant preacher,
performer of questionable miracles.

Much better that way anyway.
Better to have the charge be treason,
insurrection, or the like,
so that his death lies at the Romans' door,
and far from our temple precinct.

It was a distasteful affair,
especially those false witnesses,
disgusting types, unclean to deal with,
and expensive too.
The whole idea was Annas's, of course,
not mine.
Still, it put the cap on it,
drove home the final nail—
to coin a phrase—
in our case against the Galilean mountebank.

He never gave an inch, though—
one must give credit where it is due—
never showed the slightest sign of yielding,
cracking under pressure,
as I was convinced he surely would.
His unconscionable arrogance somehow kept him
calm and dignified, right to the end.
Indeed, it seemed, at times,
as if he were in charge,
as if this whole sordid business
was proceeding according to his plan,
not ours,
and that this "heavenly Father" of his
was close beside him every step of the way.

Ah, but that cry.
How could I have forgotten that so soon?
That aching, wondering cry he uttered
just a few moments ago:

> My God, my God,
> why hast thou forsaken me?

That ought to do the trick,
with the common herd at least.
Those words should finally convince the rabble
that his cause was Godless,

or at least mistaken,
from the start.
They will never know
that the words he spoke
were a quotation from Psalm twenty two.
None of them will ever realize
that that Psalm concludes in victory,
a song of final triumph over the enemies of God.
I must remember to alert the whole Sanhedrin
to make sure that point is kept obscure.

Some of those other things he has said
were simply amazing in their pompous self-assurance.
Imagine praying for forgiveness for one's executioners!
And that dreadful piece of nonsense
to the robber on his left hand
about being with him this very day
in paradise!
Paradise indeed!
What utter claptrap!
The closest he'll ever find himself to paradise
will be when his dying eyes behold the temple mount.
And as for making such a promise
to those depraved creatures crucified beside him,
why, such talk degrades the whole idea of paradise.
If reprobates and sinners such as these
are going to be there,
then the High Priest
will have to find some other spot
in which to spend eternity.
Ah yes, at last,
it looks as if they're going to finish them off.
There go the soldiers with the spear,
and they're breaking that one's legs
to get him down.

It is finished.

Was that what I heard just now?
Was that what he cried just as he sagged
and appeared to be giving up the ghost?
He must have meant, the jig is up,
the plot, conspiracy, has crumbled
in the end to dust.
This whole tomfoolery of posturing as Messiah
has finally reached its sad and grim conclusion.

But it seemed to me more as if he said,

It is accomplished,

as if everything that we have done,
the entire shabby process
of last night's betrayal
and this long day's brutality,
has gone according to some plan.
What an odd idea, an idiotic notion.
And yet it has recurred to me repeatedly
throughout these long proceedings.

Must be lack of sleep
that's leaving me distracted.
Must be the shock effect
of all these horrors I have witnessed—
had to watch through for the sake of God
and for the honor of his temple—
that is sending phantoms racing through my mind.
I'd better go and snatch what rest I can
before the celebration of the Passover.
I simply cannot afford
to be distracted or distraught
for those vitally important ceremonies.

Oh yes! For that fool it may well be finished,
but for me this day is scarcely yet begun.

THE FACE OF MARY

I wish it could be over.
Even though it means goodbye,
even though it means
that I will never see my son again,
at least, not until that kingdom
that he never ceased to talk about,
that kingdom that they mock him for
on the board above his battered head,
not until God's kingdom comes
and sets all this to rights.

I should have known;
had known really ever since
the angel at the well so long ago,
those words of destiny and doom
that seemed to spring
from my own lips unbidden;
ever since that moment in the cattle cave,
right after he was born,
when a knifing pain,
not only in my body but throughout my being,
warned me of great suffering to come,
of anguish deeper than my years
at that time could anticipate.
And then there was the fearful rush to Egypt
and word of all those Bethlehem babies
slaughtered without mercy.

And yet the years between,
after Herod's death,

and apart from all that business
at the temple when he was twelve years old,
the years between were happy ones.
And now another Herod,
who seems to have completed
what his predecessor failed to do.
They have a taste for blood, these Herods,
as Elizabeth, my cousin, has already learned
in tears over John, her poor dead boy.
And now my turn has come.

Funny how your mind can wander
at a time like this,
roaming back in search of happier days,
or of answers to the why and wherefore of it all.
And all the time he hangs there,
hurting, bleeding, mumbling words of comfort
—just as he always did—
even to the two who die there at his side.
I suppose it doesn't do
to think too much about such things,
that's why my thoughts go running off,
doing what they can to hide.

If only I could go to him,
if somehow I could take my cloak
and wipe the blood and sweat out of his eyes,
soothe his brow with my cool hands
as I have done so often in the past.
If he has to die,
why must it be so terribly,
why can't they let me try to ease his torment,
lift the weight from his poor pierced hands
and torn feet just for a moment?
Is there nothing that a mother can do
except to stand and watch and witness here?
Is there no limit to the callousness,

the sheer brutality that people will commit
upon each other when they are ordered to
or when the lust for blood is on them?

Thank God John is close beside me.
He's the only one who stuck it out to the end,
although I did think I caught a glimpse of Peter,
shame and guilt written all over his face,
clinging to the fringes of the crowd.
Dear John, for all his quiet ways,
was brave enough to stand with us,
offering his arm, his shoulder
and his love to Magdalen, Salome, and to me.

I wonder just what Jesus meant
when he told John I was to be his mother
and he to be my son from this day forth.
James and the other boys
have always cared for me till now,
but John has a way with him,
a way of understanding what I'm feeling
makes me glad that he is here
and will be here in the days ahead.

We'll have to start thinking about his burial.
I do pray they let us have his body back.
Tomorrow is the Sabbath
when nothing can be bought or worked on.
Maybe that wealthy looking stranger really meant it
when he offered to provide a tomb.
Funny how Jesus could always bring out
such generosity and kindness in the folk he met;
people constantly sharing food
and clothing with those who had none,
people handing out money,
just to see the happiness and hope
it could restore to other lives.

So, at the last, a gift for him.
He'll have to accept this one
because he'll have no say in the matter.

It's growing very dark.
Storm clouds such as I have never seen.
I wonder if he notices,
wonder if he cares.
He was never afraid of storms, even as a lad,
used to laugh with glee at all the crash and flash.
No laughing now,
no more laughing ever,
no more for him . . . or for me.
I wish it could be over.

THE FACE OF PETER

Here I go,
skulking around the edges of the crowd again.
Can it have been last night—
it seems like weeks ago—
that I was loitering in the shadows
of the High Priest Caiaphas's Palace,
evading those suspicious looks
and even more suspicious questions?

Why couldn't I have remembered
what he told me only a few hours earlier,
at the table, about betraying him?
Nothing seems to stick inside my head anymore.
I just sound off without thinking,
and now look where it has gotten me.
Those women with their mocking,
          Surely you were one of them.
          You sound just like a stupid Galilean.
That crowing cock,
and it wasn't even close to sunrise.
And then the look he gave as
the soldiers led him out to Pilate's residence.
I haven't wept like that since I put on
my fisherman's apron.

"Fisher of men," he called me,
back there at the beginning of it all,
when Andrew and I found him on the shore.
Some fine fisherman I turned out to be!
Last night I lost the only catch

that ever meant more than life to me.
And now he's in the Romans' net,
pinned up there like a fish hung out to dry.
Still living, though, by the way his head
and arms are moving just a bit.

Strange, the way his arms,
stretched out like that,
remind me of him speaking on the mountainside;
how he used to ask us where we thought the limits
of God's kingdom should be set.
Was it only for the priests,
the Pharisees, and holy ones?
Should the boundaries be drawn around us Jews,
shutting out all Gentiles?
Might we also allow in all the good folk,
those who tried, the best they could,
to keep God's laws and ordinances?
And then he'd spread his arms out wide,
just as if he meant to grasp the whole wide world
in his embrace, and bellow,
with a broad and beaming grin across his face,
        This wide, would you believe?
        No, even wider, wider by far than I
        or anyone can ever hope to reach.
        God's kingdom is for everyone, no limits,
        sinners too, especially sinners,
        that's why I am here today.
        For you, and you and you.

Oh no, he's looking over this way.
It's as if he's searching for me,
sifting through the crowd with his weary,
wounded, yet still tender gaze.
And those arms again, pinned down so cruelly
and yet I could almost swear they're moving,
beckoning, gesturing me closer.

Calling me to join him on that cross.
What was that he said again,
when first I called him "Christos"
on the road by Caesarea Phillipi,
about taking up the cross and following?
And I rebuked him.
Little wonder that he spoke to me as Satan.

But if I go to him they'll know me,
seize me, strip me, hang me high
there by his side.
Surely that is not what he would ask,
is asking of me. There's nothing I can do
up there to help. Surely I can be of more use
safe out here and free, able to carry on his work.
Surely it would only be a useless gesture.
And then, what of the burden
of my wife and family left
to the care of Andrew and the rest.

They are looking at me again.
Isn't that one of the palace girls
from last night standing over there,
talking to those around her
and then pointing in my direction?
Better move along, better fade back into the crowd,
get lost again, as if I never had been found,
lost as I was before I found him,
before he found me.
Who's lost now?
Got to go.

THE FACE OF SALOME

What does John think he is up to?
James, at least, had the sense to hide,
after the arrest in the garden last night.
He's probably with his cousins out in Bethany—
always was the smarter of my two boys.
But John . . .
you'd almost think he wanted to be arrested.
And crucified too, in the bargain!

A good thing old Zebedee isn't here.
He'd be yelling at the boy,
creating a disturbance,
attracting more unwelcome attention
than anything John is capable of doing.
Anyway, people probably think he is here
as a friend of the grieving family,
brought along by us women for protection
against this unruly mob of vagabonds and thieves.
No one would suspect he was one of Jesus' men,
at least, not with the way they think of Jesus here.
My John is too dreamy-eyed and gentle faced,
too soft-bearded, to ever fit the image
of a dangerous insurrectionist.

In a way I'm glad he's with us.
Poor Mary needs a man to lean on
and John has always understood such things.
He is such a gentle soul,
always thinking of others,
never of himself.

It can be a fault, you know,
that selflessness at times.
Even when I urged the two of them
to speak to Jesus on the road
about their places in his coming kingdom,
John held back and left the most of it to his brother.
Didn't help, as things turned out.
Jesus certainly blasted the two of them
with equal heaps of scorn.
I was glad he didn't turn his rage on me,
although he surely must have suspected something.

Such a long day this has been,
on our feet since the first trial
at Caiaphas's residence,
then to Herod's and to Pilate's court,
and still no end in sight.
More's the pity, I say.
Would be far better for them, for everyone,
if this terrible thing could be over
and the boys back home safe in Galilee
with their father's fishing boat and nets.

Maybe, dreadful as it sounds,
maybe this will all work out for the best
in the long run,
with things back to normal
and the old familiar routines restored.

I'm not sure I liked that statement Jesus made
about John being Mary's son from now on,
and Mary being his mother.
John already has a mother,
a perfectly good mother,
even though I say it myself, as I shouldn't have to.
Of course, poor Jesus must be delirious,
what with wounds and loss of blood,

the sun and thirst,
and now these fierce storm clouds overhead.
I'm not sure I know what he was driving at.
I'm not sure he knew either.

Maybe by tomorrow,
or the next day, after Shabbat,
we can take the road to Galilee.
God, will I be glad to see our hills and lakes again,
to listen to the dawning birdsong,
to smell the scent of wildflowers from high pastures.
Jesus should have stayed there after all,
with his multitudes and miracles.
It was the disputing in Jerusalem sealed his fate.
If only he had listened to his own words
about simple things, and stayed among them,
back where he belonged.

It's getting dark.
Can't be much longer now.
Dear God, let it be over soon,
for him, for us,
for this whole troubled city,
this troubled world.
Oh yes,
and keep my two boys safe from harm.

THE FACE OF THE DEFIANT THIEF

Sold us out, he did,
going all soft on me like that,
telling me not to mock this royal fool
who hangs between us here so meek and mild—
as if he doesn't belong with the likes of us.

Some comrade he turns out to be,
after everything we have been through together,
working the streets and alleyways,
lying in chains in prison,
even saying nothing under torture yesterday.
And now, of all things,
going over at the last minute to the other side,
finding religion
and looking for a place in paradise.

Who does he think he is anyway,
this one they title "King of the Jews"?
Messiah, too, they were shouting.
Didn't you hear the priests and Pharisees,
those gray beard, whited sepulchres,
with their fancy, tasseled robes and such,
yelling up at him, if he is the Son of God
then why doesn't he come down?

That's all I asked . . .
the same as they did really—
Why can't the poor sucker just float free
of all this cursed wood and nails
and take us both along with him?

You'd think, by now,
he'd start to realize he's done for
and not even holy God himself will rescue him.
You'd think, by now, he'd join us
in our curses and our threats.
Instead he's won my partner from me.
Instead he's shown such courage and compassion
I'm beginning to have my doubts too
about who he really is
and what he's doing up here
sharing our fate.

Maybe it's not too late.
Maybe there's still time for me.
Maybe I can catch his eye again
before this pain becomes too much for me,
before it's just too hard to draw another breath.
What was that cry?
Oh God, he can't be gone already.

But it seems as if he is,
and now they're coming to finish me off too.
Won't someone please have mercy on me?
Can anyone still forgive?
Is there room for just one more
in Paradise?

THE FACE OF THE PENITENT

O God, how much longer can this last?
At first, with all the hammering,
these big, coarse nails, and the pressure,
all that weight pulling, tearing at my wounds,
the pain seemed to be beyond belief,
impossible to bear.
But since then
it has grown steadily worse,
and worse, and worse,
and worse.
It must be over soon.

God, who would have believed
that I would ever pray for death,
I who craved excitement every moment,
fled the ancestral farm and fields,
a safe and certain livelihood,
for the devil-may-care of the hills
and scrambling mountain passes,
the cut and thrust of brigandage,
the songs and easy laughter,
ready passions of the tavern.

Yet now oblivion,
the ending of all this,
yes, even if it means farewell
to everything I have ever known,
or cherished, relished, cared for,
given heart, mind, and strength to,
even though all that be ended too,
I pray for death.

This poor fellow here next to me, though,
he looks worse off than I am.
What a beating they must have given him,
his flesh hanging in shreds like that
from the leaded cords of that Roman whip,
those wicked cuts across his brow
from that mockery of a crown.
From all I hear he was no robber,
rebel, crook, or murderer,
but a simple country carpenter
caught up in a religious dispute
with the temple.
What has he done to deserve this?

There goes Aaron again,
screaming at the Galilean.
As if he didn't have enough to bear
with all the mockery of those priests
and their hired gang of liars.
       Aaron cut it out.
       We, at least, deserve this fate,
       have earned every pang we bear
       by the hurts and loss, the griefs
       we have inflicted upon others.
       He has done nothing to merit this
       except to let his innocence lead him
       across the paths of the powerful.
       Let the man alone, for God's sake!

What was that?
Didn't he say "Thank you"?
That look he gave, those eyes!
It was as if he knew me,
saw deep into the desperation and despair,
the empty loneliness that tears me
even more than these grim,
agonizing wounds.

It was as if he looked
past all the blood and sweat,
the wear and tear of wasted years,
the placard here above my head
that tells of murder, plunder,
savage deeds and cruel fates.
It was as if he recognized
just who I am,
what I want to be
as well as who I have been,
the self that I have longed to give
and never had the reason,
or the person,
or the trust.
It was as if he loved me.

"King of the Jews"
the mockers call him.
Well such a king would be the first
could claim my loyalty, my hope,
yes, maybe even claim my heart.
Strange, really, how the pain has eased so,
since he looked over here,
since he spoke to me.
I don't suppose,
it couldn't be,
that he is blessing me somehow,
that he is actually what these pompous fools
taunt him with being, the Healer,
the Deliverer,
that One who is to come
and save and set our people free
from pain and punishment and death.

Am I slipping?
Is this slow death
first driving me out of my wits

before it drives me from this world?
Or is there in this man,
this Jesus, a royal grace,
a tenderness that has such power,
such vast enduring strength,
that it wipes out the pain,
the shame,
even the dread of what comes next,
the death that I was praying for?

> Lord,
> Lord, over there,
> yes, Jesus, Lord, remember me,
> please don't forget,
> as I will never forget you,
> Lord, don't forget me, please,
> remember me, hold me in your love,
> when you come into your kingdom.

THE FACE OF THE CENTURION

They seem a bit quieter now,
must be weakening at last,
losing all that blood
and the shock to the system
from the beatings and the nails.
Can't be much longer,
although I've heard of some who hang on,
hang up there for days.
Surely they must want to die,
get the cursed thing over with,
but their bodies won't give in,
won't let them go.

This lot look pretty near to death already.
Even their cursing and screaming—
pretty strong stuff at the beginning—
has dwindled to the occasional groan,
or another long, heaving sigh
from the one in the middle.

This is the kind of trash
I always seem to get landed with.
When there's an embassy to escort,
ceremonial parades or royal welcomes,
even some daring raid to carry out,
I end up sitting in the mess hall.
But when there's savage death afoot,
innocent blood to be shed,
or something shady to be pulled off,

it's me and my lads
who get called on every time.

They never see what they have done.
The great Lord high and mighty Pilate
sits on his Governor's seat,
pronounces verdict, signs, and seals,
but never has to watch what happens next.
He doesn't see the stripping,
hear the impact of the lead-tipped cat,
know the taste of someone's blood
and spattered skin and flesh
across the cheek and lips
as you stand by and witness
as the book requires.
He doesn't have to strain
to hold the sweating, slippery,
fouled and evil-smelling wretches down
while they heave with every ounce of strength
to avoid those piercing bloody nails.
His delicate, well-washed ears
hear nothing of their desperate shrieks,
or the coarse laughter of my troop
concealing deep disgust beneath the brutality
of mocking, torture, callousness.
"A soldier's life,"
that's what they call it.
If they only knew the half of it. . . .

This one right here now,
the one whose cloak they're gaming for,
he was a strange customer.
At first I thought him crazy,
the way he blessed the boys
while they were pounding in the nails—
some of the craziest ones do that,

deny the fact that they are being killed—
then asking forgiveness for them too.

They knew what they were doing alright . . .
getting the job done as swift as possible,
and maybe just a bit more rough than necessary,
so that it would be over quick,
the job complete, papers signed,
and they could get back to the tavern
with their execution bonus
before closing time.

But as the hours go by,
I begin to get the feeling
that far from being crazy,
he's the only sane one here.
For all the torment and the taunting,
he has answered in good grace, .
and with, amazingly, a rich tone of compassion
in his voice for everyone involved
in this, his death.

On top of that,
I have felt, throughout,
and sensed in the uneasiness of my men,
a growing, deep persuasion that we are dealing here
with something far from the ordinary round,
something uncanny,
dark yet shot with radiant light,
something which, for want of better words,
feels sacred, holy, God-like.
Each word this man has uttered,
every passing glance from those dark eyes,
has pushed me, led me further on this road.
They taunted him just now
that he had claimed to be the Son of God.
The gods I know are gods of fear and terror,

the powers of the state dressed up
to make them seem divine.
But if there be a god like this,
a god whose love goes even to the cross
with words of grace and life,
then such a god is mine,
the God I've searched for all my days.
And this man surely is his Son,
must be my Lord.
I think he's gone.
God bless him.

THE FACE OF PONTIUS PILATE

I had no business going there today;
disastrous had I been recognized,
although in that beggar's robe,
disheveled, dirt smeared look,
I doubt anyone would have believed
that I was the Roman Procurator—
not even if I bellowed my name—Pilate—
at the top of my lungs.

On the other hand,
I couldn't stay away,
had to see for my own self
what kind of ending that young Jew
would make of all his trials,
betrayals, and buffetings.
Yes, it may seem ridiculous,
but I almost half believed that
there would be some kind of miracle,
that a deliverance would take place.
No, not a rescue by his followers,
they were a pathetic lot by all accounts,
but rather an angelic intervention—
yes, something of that sort.
Hadn't he told me at the Judgment Seat
of legions from the fiery hosts of heaven
who might intervene on his behalf
if he should will them to?

And then there was
that dream last night of Portia's,

quite demented she was as she screamed at me,
right there in the Hall:
> Hands Off! Don't even lay a finger on that man
> or your name, like some grim curse, will echo
> down the corridors of history in shame and
> foul repute.

Gave me quite a turn, she did, so that,
even though I felt compelled,
by the rabble and the temple leadership,
to ignore her frightful warning—
she has these spells, you know, from time to time—
her words do echo, in my head at least,
and may have helped to drive me out
to watch the execution,
mingle with that uncouth crowd.
I wonder when she'll speak to me again.

My bodyguard stuck close, as always,
difficult to disguise them with their clean cut,
ready-to-die-for-Rome-at-any-instant look.
So their eager swords were ever near at hand.
Although I'm sure their quizzical captain
did not believe a word of my tall tale
of seeking to spy out the secrets
of the Galilean insurrection.

Anyway, there I was,
shambling along and crying out for alms
all the way out to Golgotha.
But when I got there,
when I stood at last, too late for the actual nailing—
people said he took it with a prayer—
when I stood beneath his cross,
my cross,
the Roman Army requisitioned cross
I pinned him up on,
I forgot to beg,

forgot this filthy smelling robe
that still droops from my shoulders,
forgot my roles entirely, yes,
both that of beggar and of Procurator of Almighty Rome,
and stood there feeling like a little child again.
It came to me that I had not done this to him,
but rather he had acted upon me,
that for all the purple bands edging my toga,
I was not in charge, had not been from the start.

I haven't felt like that
since the time my father told me
I had been chosen to prepare for civil governance,
or at least since my enrobing by Senatus,
with Portia, our parents, the children looking on.
And even then I felt more in control.
Something vast was happening today,
I knew it in my bones and gut although
my head was spinning like a chariot wheel.
There was a power working on that cross
that made my legions seem like feeble toys.
And I stood in the shadow there and wept.

More than that, I begged.
Oh yes, that borrowed beggar's robe,
snatched from the shoulders of a petty prisoner
as we left the palace gates,
that tattered rag had suddenly become
the perfect raiment for a moment such as this,
for a person such as I had long suspected
and now knew myself to be.
I begged, you see, to be forgiven.
In that graceless, horrifying place
where pain is king and death is stripped
of every shred of dignity I sought the boon
above all boons, the gift of grace that bears
the mending touch of love to heal
the darkest places of the soul.

And now I sit,
trying to warm myself before this brazier,
trying to nerve myself to face Portia
and the storm of mockery and rage
she will undoubtedly unleash,
trying to find again the peace
I knew for one amazingly bright moment
as he cried out,
           It is finished,
lifted his face to heaven,
and yielded up—that's how it seemed to me;
he yielded up, willingly and freely,
he gave back his life to God.

Trumpets are sounding
for the changing of the guard.
Something tells me now that far more
than the watch in this old palace
is being turned about.
Something says
I have by no means heard the last
about that lad I sent to die today
and watched give up the ghost.
Something tells me that my guard
has nothing left to watch over
because the treasure and the power,
all authority over lives and minds,
has been set loose from empire or religion,
has been set deep within that experience,
that moment that I knew there at the cross,
when all seemed given to me, all seemed new,
and I looked up and into life
right at the heart of cruel death.
And now they want to set a guard,
a watch about his grave.
Good luck to them.

THE FACE OF JOSEPH OF ARIMATHEA

Generations now
it's been in the possession of our family.
And yet, strange to tell,
no one has ever used the cave.
Came to us through marriage
at the very first, or so I heard.
I seem to remember the setting
is rather an attractive one,
a quiet, shaded garden
near the outskirts of the city.

I must choose my moment carefully,
get to Pilate while the guilt still lingers,
yet before Caiaphas can present
some dreadful scheme of his own
for the disposal of the body.
The governor is such a jelly,
swayed by whomever has spoken to him last,
and terrified of turmoil,
of anything, indeed, that might reflect
back to Rome upon his competence
or fitness for his post.

Perhaps, if Nicodemus will join me
in this overture,
the proposal will carry more weight.
I wasn't the only one, after all,
among the influential, older families,
to be a secret follower,
to find in the Nazarean teacher
all that I had been searching for
for as long as I can remember.

There were others,
I caught glimpses of them
on the fringes of the crowds.
There were even some among us
who gave dinner parties in his honor,
sought him out in private sessions,
brought loved ones to him to be healed,
or tried, at first,
before it became too dangerous,
to bend the thinking of their colleagues,
even of the high Sanhedrin
in Jesus' favor.

But the high priest and his party
would have none of it,
couldn't see beyond their fear
for their own personal positions
and hereditary privilege
to the truth that Jesus taught,
to that profound, yet simple wisdom
he distilled from the scriptures
and from this world we live in.

I wonder why he threatened them so much.
He never said those things they charged him with,
never talked of toppling Rome,
or tearing down the temple stone by stone.
It was as if they tried to hear him wrongly,
as if they listened to his words
not at all for what they said,
but for what they might be made to say,
might be twisted into saying
to condemn him.

Were they simply jealous
of his influence with the common folk?
Did they fear his miracle working powers?

Or were they just offended by the simplicity
and clear truth of everything he said,
especially when compared
to their own contrived
and convoluted teachings?
Were they afraid
because they actually heard
the word of God in what he said,
saw the hand of God in all he did,
so that he judged them just by being who he was,
or perhaps they judged themselves against him
and couldn't live with what they found
so that someone had to go?

There are others troubled here,
I'm not alone in my distress
as we stand witness to this execution.
I've caught the expressions of distaste,
of sheer disgust at all this cruelty
and savage mocking.
Even if the man were guilty
such behavior, such unseemly gloating,
would be unfitting from our leaders.
But to taunt a man like Jesus,
to fling his own words back into his face,
like salt into his wounds,
is to betray,
degrade the holy office that they hold.

"You are the salt of the earth"
I can remember Jesus saying.
As if even a few of us
could add a zest
and flavor to the whole of life,
might yet transform it.
"You are the light of the world"
he told us.

Is there any way that I can shed
even a single, solitary ray of light
into this deep, seemingly impenetrable dark?

I'll go to Pilate right away,
state my case, take my chances.
Who knows what it might lead to.
Who knows what he might shape,
even in death, out of an empty cave,
a quiet garden tomb.
Didn't I hear, one time,
that he was born in such a cave?
Didn't I hear him say that death
can hold no final power,
no true dominion?
Didn't I hear him tell that love,
God's love in us, can conquer death,
will triumph over even its grim power?
The tomb is his,
let's see what he will do with it.

THE FACE OF ANDREW

"The Last Fishing Trip," I call it
because after that we never fished again,
leastwise, we never caught another fish.

We were in Galilee,
there partly, I suppose,
because the Lord had said that he would meet us there,
or so they told us after those reports of resurrection,
but also because Galilee was home and,
after all we had seen, and not seen,
done and not done,
where else was there to go?
Anyway there we were, several of us,
sitting, gazing in the fire and talking,
reminiscing, reliving those glory days
of walking with him through the hills
and fields and country roads,
feeling ourselves part of something marvelous—
even revolutionary—
that was just around the corner
and about to dawn.
We sat there talking by the fire.

We didn't speak much of Golgotha
and the evil thing they did there, too much guilt,
I suppose, for things we were afraid even to look upon;
while the empty tomb,
all those strange appearances,
were far too confusing for any one of us
to know what could be said or made of such events.
So we were living in the past again—

the warm and distant, safely distant past—
not knowing, even caring what to do
about the present or the future,
when Peter—
Peter, my big impetuous, restless brother—
stood up and said:

> I've had enough of this, this constant talk and
> memories and questions. There's only one
> thing I know how to do and that is fishing. I'm
> going back to work.

We looked at one another,
and one by one we said:

> I'm coming too.

Well, it didn't take too long
to find the boat where we had left it many months before.
Someone, old Zebedee perhaps, had kept it up for us,
so we got the nets and launched and climbed aboard.
It was evening;
heading into the best time for fish
that part of the lake.
We used to fish all night
then sell our catch—fresh as sunrise,
gleaming, glistening, still wet—
in the crystal, early morning light.
So we set the sail and launched out on the lake.

We fished the old spots first, all tested,
tried and true: the point just off the harbor,
in back of the gray island,
the bay beyond the rocky headland—

> Just for old times' sake

as Peter said.
But the old times were all gone.
Our nets stayed empty.
Next we followed hunches.

> Why not over here?
> Or across there!
> Behind that spit.
> Between the two flat rocks.
> Follow the birds,
> the gulls will lead us to them.

The night wore on,
midnight came and went
with nothing in the boat but hungry,
wet and cold and weary bodies.

> I guess we've lost the knack of it.

James muttered:

> Maybe we were away from it too long.
> No, the fish have found new feeding places.
> We'll find them yet, just wait and see.

As the night drew on into the darkest hours,
I know that some of us began to wonder
if we were, perhaps, accursed;
if, having once abandoned all our gear,
the nets and tackle no longer knew our touch,
or cared to give results.
Whatever: it was a bleak and dreary night of it
until at last—without a word—
we turned the boat to shore again
and started, weary, to row in
just as the sun was coming up.

I can't remember now who saw him first.
One moment there was nothing there, or so it seemed,
then a figure, standing on the shore,
right at the water's edge
as if he'd waited there for us the whole night through.
Gave me quite a shock, it did.
You don't expect to meet someone
at that hour and in such a place.
I think we all were startled at the sight,
for no one said a word.

Then he called to us:

>   Hey out there! No luck, huh?

We shook our tired heads and turned thumbs down.

>   Then throw the net across the other side.

Good Lord!
Did you ever try
to tell a fisherman how and where to fish,
especially after a long, cold night of catching nothing?
We should have told him where to go,
except there was something,
something that tugged at cords
so deep within and told us to obey.

We shot the net
and by the living God
the thing near burst it was so full.
We had all begun to haul on it like madmen
when suddenly John stopped and said —
as if someone had hit him hard across the head
with the boat's rudder:

>   It's him!
>   It is the Lord!

And before we could catch breath
Peter was in the water,
swimming for shore.

We got there too,
at last, dragging the net—
we couldn't lift the thing aboard—
and found a fire set,
and food—a loaf and fish—
cooking right there,
the smell alone enough to fill
our hungry mouths with water.

      Bring us some of yours,

he said.
So we quick split and cleaned a few
and laid them on the coals.

      Now let's eat breakfast.

And he took the bread and fish
and broke them in that certain way
we knew so well.

Our minds were gone,
clean gone back to that other meal,
that upper room,
those haunting words about his body and his blood.
And so we ate.

I don't remember how it tasted—
if the fish was done or overdone,
the loaf baked through and through.
I don't remember much at all,
except two feelings:
one, a sense of flooding peace and joy,
of truly being home again,

of re-defining, re-experiencing home,
not as a place, but now a presence and a power.

The other thing was fear.
Yes, fear was even there.
You see, we didn't dare to ask him who he was;
didn't dare for fear that he would fade away
and vanish and be lost again forever.
Or that other fear,
that maybe he would stay
and we would have to follow further in his footsteps,
all the way that he had gone before.
I don't know why it was, but we knew fear,
especially at first.

Then he took Peter off along the beach
while we were finishing the scraps and cleaning up.
And when we raised our eyes again,
there was only Peter,
Peter running back across the sand and pebbles,
Peter calling to us:

> Feed my sheep!
> Feed my sheep! Feed my sheep!

That was a long time gone;
and Peter now has followed him into the distance,
feeding the flock and tending them,
as we have done since then.
They crucified Peter upside down, you know,
and glorifying God with his last, gasping breath.

And now it seems I too must follow,
when they take my shackles off
and lead me forth from here into tomorrow's early dawn.
Funny, but that fear we knew has not returned
in all the years since then. . . .

"The Last Fishing Trip," I call it,
because after that we never fished again,
leastwise, we never caught another fish.

Part 2

LENT IS . . .

Lent is a time to give up
time in reaching for eternity,
to set aside the minutes
and the hours and make living
space of time, room for the hurt,
neglect, and fear that crowd
the days so near about us,
breathing room for reverie
and solitude, sufficient real
estate to stake one's life upon,
even make a claim on the frontiers
of the beyond. Lent is a time
for mending time and shaping,
bending time toward the wilderness
whose questions clear a way
for silence, its severe
awaiting void.

ASH WEDNESDAY

Why not
Affirm yourself this Lent.
Be kind and gentle to your you.
Go walking, learn to breathe, read a book,
Know bread and wine and flesh,
Love yourself
Enough to give it
As a gift of love to life,
Or death.
Share hope with one who mourns,
Grief with one who laughs,
And rediscover all the yous
You left behind in getting to this place
From which, with ashes on your head, you go
In search of Easter.

*First Appeared in *The New Republic*, February 19, 1972.

FOOTHOLD

Long before the age
of chemical solutions
we spread ash and cinders
all across the wintry walkways
to give traction and security
on days of frost and ice.
Fairly ruined the place for
sliding on the way to school
but there was always someone who
forgot and left at least one glorious
gliding moment to elevate with wings
the daily march toward the desert.
These ashes we impose upon
our later years give traction too,
arrest the slide across and down the
slippery slope of time, ground us
against the earth of "dust thou art"
until again we can take off, arms
spread akimbo, cap and schoolbag
flying, for the moment that
will stretch beyond the garden
and across the shining river.

PENITENTIAL

There is a proper penitence
that leads across this leaning-forward season,
no mere regret or manufactured mortifying,
no self-imposed remorse about
those mild suburban sins that spot
and stain the corners of our copybooks,
rather a purging
as of earth preparing Springtime,
a melting, washing action like the rain,
a breaking up and turning over
of the soil that is the human soul,
a casting off of chrysalis
that old and wrinkled yet familiar skin
before the aching ecstasy of flight
on wings unfolding iridescence
to the new spilled light.

ORIENTING LENT

The Eastering I look for
in these steadily advancing
latter years lies far beyond
all banners, brasses, lilies banked
in resurrection rows of waxen white,
will not be forceable in any way
like golden-starred forsythia
winter cut and warmed to yield
its long stemmed foretaste
leaning into spring,
will probably, I fear,
be ushered in by pain,
the body aches of aging
and that deeper hurt that moves,
soul-wise, across time's tracing
on the place where passions dwell.
The Eastering I look for
looks for me, I'm coming to suspect,
suggests itself in soft, latefalling
snowflakes, waves in passing with
the wind through last fall's drear,
tenacious-clinging leaves along
the sycamores and leaps across
alarming walks and alleyways
and yards, shadowing my wary
tread with timelessness in shards
of strangely dark, yet dazzling
fragmentary light.

SPRING TRAINING

No trips to sunny Florida,
this camp stays right where you are
and you practice there alone,
clutching a rosin bag of ashes,
knowing a regimen of kneeling
morning, noon, and night,
of testing, stretching, pressing
to the utmost marked by sweat
and tears, the looming shadows
of defeat and weary disappointment.
Forty days of this and then,
that final purple moment
when you climb the mound and
spread your arms out wide before
the eager, clamorous throng.

*First appeared in *The Living Church*, April 15, 1984.

PINNACLE

There is a towering
deep within these forty
days that finds one—
for the most part,
and despite those daily
prayers and Bible readings—
almost completely unprepared.
These forward-tending days descend
through multilayered levels,
first of fasting resolution,
then of hard-won habit,
near the end almost of boredom
and stale customary sacrifice,
toward a point of vertigo where
someone smoothly says, "Why not?"
A winning cunning voice is heard
to urge, "Let's do it, after all!"
and, before you know the score,
you are teetering across the edge
of everything, a palm leaf
in your face, a shout of
"Hosanna!" trembling in
your eager, longing ears.
The more you suffer,
don't you see, the more you
feel entitled to a reckoning
and to your final triumph over
all the kingdoms of the world.
Beware!

JERUSALEM ROAD

A journey as long as the way
from Eden to Babel and back,
as painful as Abraham's
knifebearing sojourn with Isaac,
as daring as David's cool scramble
for stones in the brook,
as grim in its ending as train tracks
that grind into Auschwitz,
as secret with hope as a son
heading home from the war,
as full of the past and the future
as breakers that thunder to shore.

*First appeared in *The Living Church*, April 12, 1981.

PALM SUNDAY HAIKU

Creature

Dumb donkey's dream role
dancing with a load of life
dressed in green branches

Hosanna

Dusty pebbles shout,
"We recognize you, brother!"
Gates lift up your heads.

*First appeared in *The Living Church*, April 12, 1981.

PALMS OF PEACE

Are they the green and waving fronds
of triumph at the city gate,
lively now, but soon to wither,
crumble into dust?
Or are they palms that stretch,
though smashed and broken,
to embrace this withered world
and tender it to late
yet lasting life?

TEMPLE CLEANSING

Such mad scrambling
   of beggars round the thresholds
      as the shekels flew,
         denarii tumbled
in the dust, even the sacred temple coinage
                              clattered
   to the gutters from the tables of the changers
         overturned
         in his cold fury.
How the lame then learned to walk,
       even to chase after
          those rolling golden coins,
  the blind picked out the secret glint of
         copper on the cobblestones,
  the dumb set up a howling fierce commotion
    over who had grabbed what first!
Surely more sudden healing came about
   through that swift act of holy anger than
      in centuries of begging for a miracle
              about those gates.
Today again the beggars
   and the changers ply their trade
      as if miracles had never come to pass.
Healing, like anger, can prove to be a passing thing,
   while cleansing never lasts that long,
             particularly in a temple.

CHRISM

She took an alabaster box
of precious oil and spilled it for him
perfuming hair and feet
sharing a fleet, impulsive gift
of love right there right then,
no pride or low display
only the basic human need to give,
to see another's face respond—
light up in joy.

We too have alabaster boxes
to be broken in the trust
that what we share will not be judged
in terms of vain conceit,
rejoiced in rather
in the open way of One
who poured the precious oil
of his own life to make
all other gifts complete.

*First appeared in *The Living Church*, February 10, 1980.

RENDERINGS

Is it lawful
to pay taxes? Knifing
trifling terrier snatches at the heels
while the most god-awful murder hatches
crafty in the wheels of smooth despair.
Show me a coin.
Whose image does it wear?
Careful rabbi, never sharing
easy answers, ever further pressing questions
safely not to be examined
even in the private tomb of night.
Yet indictment in this very act
of bearing bony Caesar's visage
or any graven other
in the city holy to the Sinai pact.

Whose image lights
those thirty shiny coins
down in the velvet bag?
Whose copper frown warms
in your palm, deep in the loin,
place you secrete the best from harm,
until the dirty money, proper earned,
returned, can buy a discrete field of blood?
Whose alloy face can occupy
that steep and holiest of holy,
usurp the one majestic image
set when royal we formed man from mud,
pronounced him very good,
and sealed all
with the impress of approval?

Whose image on the coin,
in the palm, the bag,
the heart or groin?
Whose image? Seek it
at the core of him
who laughs with alabaster loves,
lets fly the temple doves,
turns tables toppling and stone tablets,
wines stale water into sparkling,
disrespectfully declines
to purchase death
with life,
and stretching arms for nails
wrenches all from grim Caesar,
and renders all to one.

*First appeared in *The New Republic*, April 13, 1974.

Defining—
Maundy Thursday

Maundy comes from
mandatum—a commandment
new delivered now by strong
and ready hands, ready to
gird and wash and wipe
both feet and lives
to show us all that
love takes lowliness
to heart and kneels most
readily, an art which also
brings those hands to breaking,
pouring, mending, being pierced
and molding, crafting endlessness
from tombs, grave wrappings,
guards and deadly fear.

TENEBRAE

The year's reversed
Spring's turning overturned
as, candlewise, we snuff our way
back to the steep and spreading stain
of winter's night again.

Words wound our ears
as once they wounded one
whose tears dropped dark and fast
and passion-filled in prayer
to water us a garden.

Night rules supreme
the final solitary gleam,
his star, is carried forth and hid.
We taste familiar blackness
recalling all we did
and did not do.

*Reprinted by permission from *The Cresset*: A Review of Arts, Literature, and Public Affairs, March 1982; published by Valparaiso University.

THROUGH A GLASS DARKLY
A MAUNDY THURSDAY TENEBRAE MEDITATION

For now we see through a glass, darkly . . .
(1 Corinthians 13:12, KJV)

But this is your hour, and the power of darkness.
(Luke 22:53, KJV)

The night was very dark.
Clouds must have drifted in, blotted out
the brightness of the Nisan moon of Passover.
You could hardly see your hand
before your face, I recall,
and as we left that upper room, regained
the narrow street and then set off toward
the Mount of Olives, shadows seemed to settle in,
fall into place beside us. We walked
amid a growing throng of shadows.
Yes, the night was very dark.

Hard it was, you realize, to tell
just where this blackness came from;
whether these were shadows of the night or
of the mind and heart. We looked at one another,
and it was as if we saw through darkened lenses.
We looked ahead at him—our Lord and Leader—
and a murkiness crept in upon our sight.
Was it the gloom of ignorance we felt?
For we had thought, at last,
that things were moving full ahead,
that Jesus really had a plan not just to save
his life and ours, but to redeem the land,

to bring back Holy Israel from the dark obscure
into the light of freedom, independence
from the pagan heel of mighty Rome.
We had thought his entry to Jerusalem
with cheering crowds, cries of "Messiah!" and
flailing palms, would signify the time of acclamation,
his coming at the last into his kingdom and his reign.
We had hoped that we, his closest friends
and followers, would have a role in all of this,
would find a space within the new regime
would know after the months and years of hardship—
traveling the dusty roads and villages
with nothing but the clothes we wore,
the sandals on our feet—that we would meet
at last our due reward, could count on places
by his side when he assumed the throne
that he had moved toward across these hard
and testing intervening years.
Our minds, you see, were shadowed,
somehow darkened by the hopes we had been
born with, so that we only saw the freedom
we had hoped for; could not even glimpse
the fuller, truer liberty he lived out
by our side and in our company.
We heard his teaching, hung upon his every word,
or so we thought, and yet these words passed
through a filter, took on darkness from the shade
within our minds. And so we saw him only,
as it were, "through a glass darkly."

There was another darkness
dogged our footsteps on that walk.
It was the dark of fear, the sheer deep pit of
terror opening again before our feet, behind our backs,
as we remembered his last words at the supper table,
words of being broken and poured out;
as our reluctant, sluggish minds yet insisted

on connecting words like these with other sayings
spoken here and there amid the many conversations on
the road; shocking words about a cross, and suffering,
about a death that must be taken up and lived through;
even worse, about such things waiting also for
his followers if they were true to him.
We used to disregard such talk, set it aside, tried
our very hardest to forget such things, to hide from them.
But then that night the whole idea came home again
to roost, like a recurring nightmare, when Judas left
so strangely just before the broken bread, the cup.
Why did we glance about so nervous as we left,
scurry across the open spaces, utter scarce one word
as we approached the place, Gethsemane?
Why did we huddle silent in the cover of the bushes,
fail to join him in his prayers, and then fall asleep
like weary wandered sheep from sheer exhaustion
so that when he was arrested we were
only half awake? We were afraid.
The dark blind of fear had been drawn down upon
our timid souls and we could see him only,
as it were, "through a glass darkly."

An even deeper dark was there, a blackness
hard to spell out even to oneself, yet hanging
like a pall across what happened on that night.
Not only ignorance and fear were there,
but sin itself—that twisted serpent "self"—
had entered in and spread its deadly poison into
all we thought and saw and did.
You see, if this, then, was the end:
if these sounds of marching feet, calling voices
on the wind, clashing swords and spears, flashing torches
in the distance, meant that he must face defeat, must now
taste the bitter failure of his vision, the full
weight of the revenge of the authorities;
then it's "every man for himself."

"Maybe this darkness is a friend after all.
Maybe there is still one chance to creep away,
escape the Roman net and get back home again
to Galilee, refuge with my family and friends."
So we thought; and we all fled.
We joined that darkness which had pressed us
all around, gave ourselves up to its embrace,
and in ignorance and fear and love of self
abandoned him and all we held most dear,
ran for our miserable lives and now
are gathered here to mourn and
ask each other, "Why?"

The whole thing seemed to happen,
don't you see, in the pitch dark, among
deep shadows. What was it he said to them again?
"But this is your hour and the power of darkness."
Shadows surround us still.
It is as if we have been living
in a darkened world of late. And while
we gather here and wait, not knowing
what or who it is we wait for,
we all share a sense of seeing
everything as if it were perceived
"through a glass darkly."

HE TOOK A TOWEL
MAUNDY THURSDAY MEDITATION

*Then he poured water into a basin, and began to
wash the disciples' feet, and to wipe them with the
towel with which he was girded.*
                                    (John 13:5, RSV)

He took a towel and washed their dusty feet.
An ordinary, routine act of hospitality,
customary for that time and place,
an act that bore within itself the message
of a warm and friendly greeting and of welcome
to one's guests. And yet an act that was to be
performed not by the host, but by a servant
or a slave, one set there by the door for this task,
one accustomed, don't you see? to appearing
on his bended knees in front of other human beings,
one who might properly and conveniently touch
and wipe and cleanse the body of another
without offense, without the slightest suggestion
there of intimacy, without even being noticed.
In other words one who knew his menial place in life
and could assume it, or so we assume, by instinct.
Shoeshine boy in a land where feet,
not shoes, had to be made to glisten.

He took a towel and washed their dusty feet.
Yet while those feet were being soothed,
refreshed from that long day's weary
and overheated journeying, what turmoil
must have been arising in the minds,
and yes, the souls of those proud Jews,
seeing their teacher, master, hoped-for Savior

kneel before them, each in turn,
and serve them as a slave.

Who should have done the job after all?
That question must have raced across their minds
as they assembled. Was not Judas charged
with money matters, hiring and paying for
necessary servants and the like?
Or what about those two he had already sent ahead
to make all the arrangements for the meal?
Couldn't they be held responsible?
Someone must have slipped up somewhere.
Someone, surely, could have hired a slave or two
instead of creating such an awkward, embarrassing situation.
Or, failing all of this,
someone surely might have volunteered.
Not me of course, with my position in the group,
my dignity to be maintained,
but surely one of the younger ones,
one of the newer ones,
one of the women, perhaps, surely someone. . . .
He took a towel and washed their dusty feet.

He takes a towel and washes our tired feet,
unbinds the cramping cords that rein us in,
removes the awkward leather of protection and display,
the wool for warmth and decency, then wipes
our weary feet to make them cool and fresh and clean.
Can we accept it? That's the question.
Can we discover for ourselves tonight the true humility
and genuine affection that comes from being served
by one we worship and adore?
Can we believe, can we even recognize
the amazing revelation that such a simple,
humble, gentle act will yet expose the very heart
of the Divine? Can we find in all of this a God
who sees the tensions, petty vanities, hostilities

that set us all apart, who knows the self-erected walls
of pride and fear dividing all his children,
a God who realizing we can only be united, brought together
once again by an act of great self-offering and self-denial,
an act of which not one of us is capable,
performs the necessary deed himself,
strips and girding with a towel
says to you and me, "Your feet are tired, child;
take off your shoes and let me soothe them"?

Then, "This is my example" says the Lord,
"As I have done to you, so you must do."
To wash the weary, dusty, bruised
and bloodied feet of sisters and of brothers,
of the homeless and the hungry, of family and friends,
of our neighbors and our rivals—
even those whose hands you would not wish to shake.
To wash their weary feet and then to dry them,
gentle now, with your own garment,
then finally to welcome and to seat them,
every hungry, hurting, lost and lonely child of God,
to seat them cleansed, forgiven, loved,
restored around a table that is spread,
around this holy table where the Lord of all
reigns at his royal feast.

So let us learn to greet our neighbor with the touch
of peace, the touch that cleanses, soothes,
refreshes, and brings life since it is the peace of God
we pass and not our own.
Let us turn to one another in the Lord,
and thus turning become partners,
welcome partners for the feast he has prepared;
the feast at which, so long ago,
he took a towel and washed their dusty feet.

THOMAS'S TESTIMONY
A COMMUNION MEDITATION

*How I have longed to eat this Passover with you
before my death.*

(Luke 22:15, NEB)

Yes, they always said I questioned everything—
too much for my own good, was the way they
used to put it.
Although, since that evening in the upper room when he
offered me his hands and side, the nail prints, spear wound
to touch and know, I've never doubted him again.
And yet, I still have questions.

For instance, what he meant when he told us
how he'd wished to eat that supper with us just
before he died. "How I have *longed* . . ." he said;
as if that was a moment he had lived for all his days.
"How I have longed to eat this Pesach with you all
before I die." It gave us quite a shock, I can tell you,
him talking again like that about his death.
But it was the longing that puzzled me at the time;
still catches, tugs the tangled cords of memory
after all these many years. "How I have longed. . . ."
What could the Lord have meant by that
expression of deep yearning?

Might it have been because he knew the goal
was now within his reach, that after three hard years
of testing, trial, stress, and many disappointments,
giving, always giving, pouring out his mind, his heart,

his very soul, spilling forth so readily the vibrant life
that was within him in acts of healing, feeding, loving,
might it have been with some relief he caught sight
of the end of his long journey, glimpsed the goal which,
fearful though it was to us, to him would mean fulfillment
of his task, the long expected climax and conclusion
of his pilgrimage? Was that, perhaps, why Jesus said
he longed to share the feast with us, because
it meant that all was nearly over?

Another thought. Could he have seen this supper
as a fond farewell; one final feast with all of us before
he faced the end alone? We certainly had shared enough,
had plenty to remember and be thankful for that night.
So much had happened since he called us from the boats,
the sheds and shops, the hillsides of sweet Galilee,
so many miles of journeying, so many mouths fed,
miseries relieved. Everywhere we went, especially at first,
there were crowds, crowds wanting something, food,
freedom, a future maybe, something they could hope for,
live for, shape their battered lives around
and start to dream again. Mostly they came, I think,
because he loved them and could tell them so, yes,
even those vast, milling throngs; there was a touch,
a sense, a spirit moving in, across, among those mobs
of eager people, told them here at last they had a man
who was concerned, not for himself, who was not
out to get himself elected, but who cared for every
single one of them: children and tottering old dames,
lepers, whores, soldiers, robbers;
I've seen them all transformed by seeing him.
So anyway, perhaps it was the thought of all we'd shared,
the memories, relationships we had built up, he wanted,
then, to celebrate, to gather all together in one last
and glorious evening of true fellowship before he said,
"Farewell" to us, the twelve who had walked
with him all the way.

And yet I think that there was even more
than this within that longing. He said it
with such passion, I have never, even yet, been able
to forget those words and just the way they sounded.
"How I have longed to eat this Passover
with you before I die."
Could it have been that he too was unsure,
that although he knew the fundamental fact
that he must die, he did not understand precisely how
and why this had to be fulfilled? It seemed to me as if,
in all he did that evening at the table, he too was finding
meaning and enlightenment, as if, in breaking bread
and pouring wine, our Lord himself was being led—
as we were through him—
into a new and richer comprehension,
into a full and final revelation that this, of course,
was why it must be so—that only as a grain of wheat falls
to the ground and dies can it arise again and bring forth
ripe new grain to form the loaf that feeds a hungry world.
Yes, I believe it dawned on him—as he was doing it—
that bread, in being broken, is available, and being shared
becomes a part of many bodies, many lives; multiplies
itself in twelve or twenty, twenty thousand ways, and soon
is irresistible, a mighty and united host of servants
for the kingdom. And with the cup,
so clear a symbol of his blood in that red wine,
he saw, as we did, that his life, poured forth, would seal
a new commitment, would form upon
the altar of God's grace a whole new covenant
that will replace the ancient,
worn-out slaughter of the animals with one complete
and final act, the sacrifice of God's own son
to show the world, to show us all the height
and depth and majesty, the eternal glory of God's love,
which gives itself forever, or until we come,
at last, and offer up our own lives in return.
So, as the meal progressed, we saw the Father

and the Son converse together in his actions and his words.
We watched the faith take shape, the kingdom-yet-to-be
assume its royal form, its sacramental lineaments.
We all were witnesses at the birth
of a new era, a new creation.

What followed afterwards, of course, is history.
It shattered me—the whole thing was too much.
And at the cross I had completely lost already all
I had seen and heard and tasted in the upper room
the night before. I lost it all.
And if it were not for his love, his grace
that sought me out behind locked doors, called me
to touch and then believe, I would not be here
at your humble table ready now with you, to break
the bread and pour the wine as he did years ago.
Yet I am here; here to tell you what I know,
what I remember of that night and even more,
what I believe will happen here and now as you and I
take bread and wine together in his name.
For it is with great longing that I too have longed
to eat this Passover with you.
Now in his name, and in his risen presence—
let the feast begin! AMEN.

FOUR-LETTER-WORD TREE

His word
at the last
turned wood to him
carved in a cross.
They held
his word against him,
pressed Word-made-flesh
on word-made-wood
and, pinned him
nailed him
to it.
All this
to prove that love
is more than word or
wood, than skin and bone—
is rise and walk
heal and hope
and live.

THE LAST MIRACLE

What did you, could you think
as they pounded through your open palms
forcing coarse, bloody iron nails
to sink deep into the splintered wood?

Did you feel the grasp of panic,
that sudden, stomach-wrenching sense
that this, at the very last, is it—
no further chance of changing, turning back?

Were you, perhaps, bewildered,
having hoped, despite defiant words,
for at least one late and minor miracle
on your own behalf, considering all the rest?

Did flooding fear compound with rage and hate
at the sheer blind brutality of soldiers,
fellow sons of God, treating you
like meat to be hung raw in a butcher's window?

Or dare we yet believe what was written,
that your concern was, even at the end, to shield,
to plead the cause of all who wield the whips
and crushing hammers of this crucifying world?

*First appeared in The Living Church, March 12, 1982.

TRADE QUESTIONS

Early and late
you came to know—most intimate—
the rough and ready artifacts
of your trade as carpenter.
You must have crafted
many a manger in the sawdust
and the shavings of the shop
at Nazareth.
Did they recall to you the stories
of your humble, yet bewildering birth,
those shepherds, those strange kings?
The tables you constructed,
might they have, in any way,
foreshadowed one rich table where
your hands learned other skills
the working tools a cup,
a loaf of bread?
And when you built a house
or stable, hammered cross beams,
T-beams solid into place,
what phantoms traced their way
across your youthful mind
engrossed with all the stresses
of your ancient craft?

Holy Saturday

The echoes of this intervening day
tremble between bloodshed and birth.
Full Friday's passion now is laid away.
These hours are for the proving of its worth.
In darkness will it ripen to a gay
garden scene of festival and mirth,
or in the deadly juices of decay
dissolve into the daily dust of earth?

*First appeared in the *Anglican Theological Review*, Volume 57, Number 1, January 1975.

PROCURATOR

The questions on this incident
resolve themselves in two basic directions.
Who took the body? And how?
As to the first, it must have been
his followers, plotting to claim him
risen from the dead and leave us stripped
of any evidence against. But as for shifting
that vast rock—already rolled and stopped
in place—terrifying our best guards into
a tale of angels, earthquakes, lightning,
carrying the body, minus grave bands,
to a hiding place which all our searching,
frantic, does not find . . . since when could
stupid fisher folk and veritable paupers
command such skills as these?
There is something more behind!
Some movement bigger, far, than we have
yet suspected that must lead, as all such do,
to wild rebellion, bloody swords. Pity
that a man of peace and innocence,
as he appeared to be, should be misused
in death! Pity that this god-forsaken race
cannot accept our Roman justice and learn
to live in calm prosperity with all the rest!
Pity . . .

*Appeared in *Presbyterian Survey*, April 1987.

SUNRISE SERVICE

Six-thirty may be far too late
to catch this day's first beams but
Easter too seems slow upon the scene
this year, besides, five-thirty would be
pushing faith a little far,
not faith in God to raise the dead,
you understand, but faith in all the rest
of us to rise from warm, familiar beds
and witness the event.
Anyway, the sun had not yet risen past
the rooflines, so our open, well-protected
inner courtyard was still cold
and deeply shadowed. The birds,
of course, were up already and while
below we shivered through the readings,
songs, and prayers, a fledgling sermon,
two of them—robins, I believe—sat perched
on gable ends across our slowly sunlit cloister
bracketing our chill efforts in cascading endless
streams of clear, uncluttered praise.

*Appeared in *Presbyterian Survey*, April 1988.

EGG ROLLING

Before the days of brightly
packaged dyes and decorating kits
we'd boil them long and hard in vinegar
and cochineal attaining pale and random
colorings then, after Calvin's kirk,
carry them off, with salt and pepper, to
Linlithgow Loch or other nearby slopes
to try them till they broke.
We used to vie to see
whose egg survived the longest
but speedily grew tired of cautious
tumbling along the cushioned turf, began
to toss them in the air, then trap them
just before they hit the ground. You
had to catch them right, with your
hands in motion down towards the grass
or they could smash against your palms
and the game was over.
Hunger and the cold Scots air of
April would eventually win out, and
the family all clustered round to peel
and bite into the battered relics of
our contest. A taste of resurrection
on the tongue, between the lips,
in the cold, bruised, salt-and-peppered egg,
its rich and textured blending of
the yolk and white, the creamy and
the clean, the life laid down and then
passed on, and of the family
who laugh and squabble round an ordinary
royal feast in unexpected ecstasy.

First Sunday

And was that a rising like bread, or like mountains
Explosive like ball over fence, bloom in Spring,
Or steady, relentless, as waves in the ocean,
Or steeples on churches, or gull's soaring wing?

Or perhaps it was human, like waking in April
With sun on your face, and a foretaste so wild,
And a spring in your marrow no winter can frost-kill,
And the light lifting lilt in the eyes of a child,
And the lilt in the eyes of a child.

HOPE WEED

Our Christian symbols seem, at times, not quite
appropriate to the meaning that they bear.
For instance, take the Easter lily, white
and fragile sign of resurrection. Rare,
its graceful silent trumpet greets the light
of March or April only under glare
of florists' lamps, unnaturally bright.
You never find them in the open air
before July. A better flower for Easter Day
would be, as every angry gardener knows,
the dandelion, seeded by the gay
abandoned wind that, as it listeth, blows.
No matter how we weed out every stray,
digging as deep, the root still deeper goes.
And when, at last, we quit and go away,
the rain falls, and a host of fresh bright foes
stands resurrected, and the garden glows.

*First appeared in *alive now!*, March 1976.